THE
ALZHEIMER'S
GUIDEBOOK

THE
ALZHEIMER'S
GUIDEBOOK

SHERRI LARGENT

ARPress
ILLUMINATING IDEAS
EMPOWERING VOICES

ARPress
45 Dan Road Suite 5
Canton MA 02021
Hotline: 1(888) 821-0229
Fax: 1(508) 545-7580

Ordering Information:
Quantity sales. Special discounts are available on quantity purchases by corporations, associations, and others. For details, contact the publisher at the address above.

Printed in the United States of America.

ISBN-13:	Softcover	979-8-89356-495-2
	eBook	979-8-89356-494-5

Library of Congress Control Number: 2024902960

*I would like to give special recognition to
all my patients and their families from whom
I have learned so very, very much. They have
given me a deeper insight to the very special
world of someone with Alzheimer's and I thank them.*

Sherri

PREFACE

I, the writer of this book, was a Registered Nurse who worked in an Alzheimer's/Dementia facility for nine years, which housed approximately 50 patients on a daily basis. The names in this book are fictitious. Names and scenarios are not in any way related to each other. Suggestions and comments are from myself. They are based upon the actions, responses and comments presented to me from those people with Alzheimer's/Dementia and their families. I have tried to cover a variety of situations. Some you may or may not encounter. I can only hope they help you to understand and respond to this illness with a little more clarity, a little more insight and a little more understanding.

CONCERN FOR THE FUTURE: One of my greatest concerns is what the future holds for placement of these individuals. If they cannot be taken care of safely at home, then our only other alternative is to place them in a facility that will be a home away from home-----a place that will care for them until the end of their life, with the best care possible. With the rate of Alzheimer's growth, how many facilities will be available to tend to their needs.....or better yet... how many will be equipped with the knowledge and understanding of this disease in order to care for their needs with compassion, safety and understanding?

Note: All scripture verses are taken from Life Application Bible – New International Version – NIV – Zondervan –1991

Table of Contents

THE ALZHEIMER'S GUIDEBOOK

There is always a possibility that you or I will develop Alzheimer's in the future...but there is even a greater possibility that someone you or I know has already started with the first symptoms of this dreaded disease.

At the time of this writing, I was a registered nurse for about 20 years and had worked in the hospital setting, a very busy walk-in clinic and hospice. As with most jobs, I gained experience and knowledge from each position I held, and each position led me to a different aspect of the nursing field. Not many people can say they loved their jobs, but I did. I loved nursing, and I still do. However, my most enjoyable, and I have to say "most rewarding" position, was taking care of Alzheimer's/Dementia patients.

I had the privilege of caring for Alzheimer's/Dementia patients five days a week, eight hours a day, for a period of almost nine years. In most cases, I was able to be there when they arrived at the facility (which specialized in the care of those with Alzheimer's/Dementia), during their stay, and sadly when they passed.

I listened, I watched, I learned and I sought to provide the best possible care for them – with the help from the medical team I worked with. My heart went out to the families as well as the care-workers that helped provide for their needs. The longer I was with them and the more I saw, I realized how many people needed help in dealing with and caring for a loved one with this disease. Through my experiences, with the help of others and by the Grace of God, I learned a multitude of ways to help all of those involved; the patient, the family, friends and caregivers. I kept thinking that if only others knew what to do, what to expect, and how to handle it, their lives would be so much better –so much easier for their loved one and themselves. They needed knowledge and support. So---I wrote down as much information as I could and put it into this guidebook. The stories are true, and some are very similar. The names are fictitious. My recommendations are based solely upon the knowledge I obtained from actual experiences and observations during the time I spent working with and caring for these patients and their families. Now… I hope this helps you.

Forty years ago, I purchased a book written by Dr. Spock that was published with the intent of helping young mothers learn what to expect with the birth of their newborn, how to take care of them, and how to deal with all the problems that go along with raising and caring for young children. It was very helpful, specifically informative, and never having children before, I don't know what I would have done without it. I referred to that book regularly.

This book is written with similar intention. It is written in hopes of reaching the rapidly growing population of families with Alzheimer's disease. I hope it will be a helpful tool in providing you with the knowledge of the care required, as well as understanding the signs and symptoms of someone with Alzheimer's/ Dementia as their disease progresses. By sharing with you actual patient and family scenarios, and then giving you helpful advice on how certain situations were managed, my hope is that you, too, will have a greater understanding of how to handle things if given that similar event. Most of all, I trust this information will make it easier for you—whether it is for the hands-on care required or for help in coping and accepting. I hope you will regularly return to the information in this book and use it as a guide during the care of your loved one.

Basically, Dementia is a general term that is used to refer to an impairment in the intellectual ability of someone. It portrays a dysfunction such as memory loss, paranoia, impaired thinking, perhaps concentration, as well as changes in sleep patterns or even depression. It can be caused by any of various problems: occurrences in the vascular system, alcohol abuse, infectious disease process, tumor, Alzheimer's, or certain drugs and/or their abuse. Dementia may start slowly over a period of months to years, depending on its origination, cause and/or treatment.

Alzheimer's is a form of dementia, so-to-speak. It is a continual progressive disease caused by the wasting away of certain parts of the brain. As it progresses, the symptoms present as irreversible memory loss, speech and sleep disturbances, intellectual dysfunction, disorientation, behavior changes, problems with walking and balance, changes in swallowing and eating, all depending on its progression. It is said that brain cells are destroyed. As the destructive pattern progresses, the disease worsens and, sadly to say, will lead to the demise of the person. However, with each person, the time span can be different.

As of this writing, there is no cure for Alzheimer's. Scientists are continually working on a cure, but as with other major illnesses in our world, one has yet to be found. What they HAVE found, and continue to explore, are new and innovative ways to help with the symptoms of the disease. One way is the use of medications. Prescribed medications can alleviate various symptoms with which the patient may present. Some medications can even delay, to a certain extent, the progression of the disease process---while others can hinder an Alzheimer patient's attentiveness. Therefore, be sure to discuss the use of any medications thoroughly with your doctor, and don't be afraid to ask questions.

We must not forget that individuals with Alzheimer's are not limited to the disease of Alzheimer's alone. They, also, are subject to the flu, colds, heart problems, high blood pressure, diabetes, cancer, etc., like you or me. Being attuned to the signs and symptoms of these additional illnesses is another aspect of caring for someone with Alzheimer's. Dependent upon how far Alzheimer's has progressed in your loved one, will have a huge impact on the treatment you will want rendered. So… …I encourage you to sit down with your family and/or your doctor to discuss how often, and for what reasons, you want your loved one to see a doctor.

NOTE: The following short stories are incidents that actually occurred.

Part I

Introduction

CHAPTER 1

STORY OF MARTHA

Martha's symptoms began while she was living at home on her own. She was a well-to-do woman who was able to care for herself. However, something was changing, and she knew it. Her memory was not the same. At first it was simple, small things, like forgetting to feed her cat or forgetting where her car keys were. Then it became more noticeable. One day she went to the store and forgot her way home. She sat for hours in her car. Luckily she remembered the way back.

She then started having problems writing checks to pay her bills. She would sit down to write a check and forget how to fill one out. There were times that she would put things on the stove, forget about it, and find out later that the food was burning. Other times she would find that the food was partially cooked or supper was started, but never finished. Her family did not realize there was a problem, but she did. This little lady, God bless her, was able to recognize her situation and take action. She realized that the problem was getting out of control, and before she could no longer be "in charge" of things, she confided in her family. She told them that she knew something was not right and wanted to get things in order before it was too late. All legal documents, medical directives, power of attorney, home ownership, trust's, CD's, etc., were taken care of…and just in time. Soon after, Martha began to show more symptoms of her dementia and was later diagnosed with Alzheimer's.

TIP-- It is important to openly discuss your concerns with the doctor and family members. The prognosis may or may not be pleasant, but knowledge and understanding is necessary in order to help you prepare for the inevitable.

CHAPTER 2

THOMAS

Thomas' episodes of wandering began almost 7 years after he was diagnosed with Alzheimer's. His wife was taking care of him at the time. He usually slept very well at night. As time went by, his wife noticed that he was going to bed later and later each night, and it was becoming more difficult to get him into bed. She was losing sleep because she had to be up with him, not trusting what he would get into to. One night she had fallen asleep in a chair and awakened to a cool breeze blowing across her. To her dismay, Thomas was nowhere to be found. She saw that the front door was open and it was very dark outside. She went up and down the street looking for him, but could not find him. She called the police and an alert was placed. Thomas was found in the middle of a major intersection almost a mile from home. He was safely returned home and some changes were made for his safety. Locks were placed high up on all the doors in the house so he could not reach them. Needless to say, Thomas managed to get a chair and unlock the doors to go outside. Several times he was found in neighbor's yards 4 to 5 blocks away. Episodes like these continued and his wife knew she could no longer take care of him. Concerned for his safety, as well as her health, he was placed in a locked facility for Alzheimer's.

CHAPTER 3

HARRY

Harry had started with signs and symptoms of Alzheimer's about 5-7 years ago. He and his wife were in the midst of enjoying their retirement together when his wife realized something was changing. They would have frequent visits with their grand-children and Harry would forget he had seen them. He would repeatedly ask when were they going to visit them, and was told they had just seen them a couple of days ago. Then the episodes of forgetfulness began to escalate. Harry would leave to go to the store and forget how to get back home. His wife would receive phone calls from someone at the local grocery store or gas station telling her to come pick up Harry. At other times, his wife would be home worrying when he did not return, and family members would begin their search, only to find him at the park, on the side of the road, or sitting in the laundromat or supermarket. Each time he did not know why he was there. Several times the police had to be called to help find him.

Harry continued to deny his problem of memory loss and/or confusion. Whether it was denial or just his inability to know, is not known. His wife had to finally refuse to let him drive or leave the house alone, which made him very angry. His anger often led to aggressive behavior and threats. With his bouts of rage, she had a hard time keeping him safe, let alone herself. She continually tried to explain to him about his behavior and forgetfulness, but Harry could not understand. Many times to prevent his anger from escalating further, she would try to change the subject and lead him into another area of discussion. This "re-direction" technique was not always effective.

Other problems began to surface. He would refuse to shower for days, have periods of wetting his pants and would not let his wife remove the wet clothing. He would refuse to take his medication and began complaining about the food they were eating. At times, he would leave the stove on or the water running in the sink. He had periods of paranoia, insisted someone was trying to kill him and became very suspicious of his wife. With his episodes of uncontrollable anger, his wife finally realized she could no longer care for him. She shared her concerns with her family and spoke to his doctor and their pastor, as well. All agreed that for her safety and Harry's, placement options had to be considered. For quite some time, she felt guilty for having to place him in an Alzheimer's facility. As time passed, she realized it was the best thing she could have done for him and herself.

"Come to Me, all you who are weary and burdened, and I will give you rest." Matt. 11:28 NIV

PART II

MEDICAL DECISIONS

CHAPTER 4

Choosing a Doctor

Consulting your family doctor is an essential part in the care of your loved one. If your family member has a specialist, you may want to continue under his/her care. If your loved one is seeing a doctor for medications that control certain behavior problems that have already been identified, such as a psychiatrist or neurologist, it is important to know his/her professional role in the care of your loved one, as well as their experience with the disease. Whatever your decision, try to find a doctor that you are truly satisfied with, one you trust, and one that is familiar with your family member and Alzheimer's.

I say this because I have been involved with doctor visits that have been most dissatisfying. Unfortunately, at certain stages of the disease, many Alzheimer's patients will not sit still long enough to be examined. They may become nervous, scared, or even aggressive, and will not follow instruction. Some don't remember what a doctor is, and may not realize that someone is trying to help them. This can lead to unexpected behavior. If this were to happen, going into a doctor's office for a visit may become complicated for the doctor, the patient, and you. So, make sure you feel confident with the doctor you have chosen. One that will be able to take the appropriate time for a good assessment, and be compassionately understanding.

***HILDA was having trouble with drainage from her ear and kept holding her hand over her ear as if in pain. Her mood had changed and sometimes it was difficult to get her cooperation. This was unusual for her. An appointment was made to have her ear examined by a doctor. After ten minutes of trying to have Hilda sit long enough for the doctor to examine her, he said, "Why did you even bring her here? I can't examine her. She needs to go to the ER."

***VICTOR needed a dressing change to his foot. I tried to raise his foot up, but he was not cooperating very well. He looked at me as if I was annoying him, not realizing I was trying to help him. I said, "Victor, could you help me lift your foot so I can make sure it is ok?" He replied, "Yeah," with a smile, "so I'll kick you in the face." Victor meant no harm, but he also meant what he said. Needless to say, I did not check his foot at that time. The next attempt, however, was successful. Some doctors may not have time for occurrences like this, or they may not understand the actions of someone with Alzheimer's. It also could get a little costly for the family to make two trips to accomplish something, versus one trip to a doctor who understands Alzheimer's-- or one who is aware of and prepared for, a possible behavior problem.

***JOSH was having trouble chewing his food. It was noticed that he was keeping the food in his mouth a lot longer and "playing" with it. This was not his norm. Sometimes he would spit out the food. Through observation and monitoring, it was apparent he was having discomfort with eating. An appointment was made for him to see a dentist. After two separate dental visits, with two different dentists, a difficult time in the dentist chair dealing with Josh's anxiety, distress to the family, and disruption in the dentist office waiting room, we finally found a dentist that came to the facility. He examined the patient and suggested the use of certain medications prior to making the needed visit to his office. The advice was taken, medication administered, and Josh was taken to the dentist office where his cavity was addressed. Preparation for times like this, is prudent. Of course, there will be times in the advanced stages of Alzheimer's that a dental visit with a scenario such as this, may not be the best choice.

TIP--If for any reason your loved one needs to go to the hospital, I highly suggest that they are not left alone in the waiting room, the ER, or even their hospital room, if admitted. If left unaccompanied, there is always the chance they may wander, fall out of bed or leave the facility, as the hospital staff is not always available to monitor them. Also, your loved one will not be able to answer any questions adequately when asked by the hospital staff who may not know your loved ones history or be familiar with Alzheimer's disease.

NOTE: Martha was able to openly discuss her future with her family—luckily in time. She sold her home and put money away for the intended purpose of her care sometime in the future. She moved in with family and together they enjoyed life for a number of years.

Hilda was seen by a wonderful doctor who came to her place of residence, examined her with patience, and prescribed the right medication to care for her ear. Victor's wound healed, under the guidance of a physician. Josh returned to his normal eating habits.

CHAPTER 5

Medical Directives

Medical directives are legal forms that have been prepared ahead of time that document the wishes of a person and their medical treatment. Some medical directives are as follows: living will, health care surrogate and DNR (DO NOT RESUSCITATE). There may come a time when the patient and/or the family may need to decide if hospitalization will be a choice for potential health problems and/or what steps they want to take for care and treatment if they are faced with a life-threatening incident. If the patient is oriented and still able to make his/her own decisions, there usually is no problem. However, if they are not mentally capable to make those decisions, it then becomes the family's responsibility. This in itself, although often done, could be very difficult. If directives are prepared in advance, and prior to any incident or emergency, with the patient's wishes fulfilled, it could alleviate difficult decisions for the family members at a later date. Everyone will be under enough stress, so handling delicate matters like these ahead of time, may help to prevent future added stress. Talk it over with each other. See what works for you. You may also want to consult your doctor and/or a lawyer.

TIP—Medical directives are not only meant for people with Alzheimer's. All families would benefit by making pre-planned decisions on their directives when it comes to end of life, hospitalization and life saving measures. Some of us tend to put things off, and when the time comes, you or your family may wish you hadn't.

CHAPTER 6

CARE OPTIONS

Several things will affect the type of care you choose for your loved one:

.....decisions the patient or family have made pertaining to his/her care

.....how much money you have to work with or insurance available

.....availability of a family member to care for him/her at home

.....safety (for the patient as well as the spouse/caregiver)

.....stage of Alzheimer's the patient is in or their prognosis

If there are several family members involved, it is recommended that everyone openly discuss how your loved one is going to be cared for. You may decide that the care will be shared amongst each of you. It may work out that someone who is home and not working will care for him/her in the daytime and someone else may do the care in the evening. If both are working, and need to work, there may be money put away, insurance or savings that could be used to hire a qualified caregiver for the daytime. You may even consider an Alzheimer's daycare facility for the daytime, and care for him/her yourself at night. Some people will be fortunate enough to have money that will cover the cost for a live-in caregiver or a home health person 24 hours a day. There are others who are less fortunate and will have more difficulty in finding a solution, due to the cost involved.

If the spouse is retired and the patient is in the early stages of Alzheimer's, it may work well for the spouse to keep him/her at home as long as he/she can provide the care and maintain a safe environment. The availability of money, insurance, Medicare, etc., will play an important role in the decision, as well as how far the disease has progressed. Another option is placement in a nursing home, or a facility that specializes in Alzheimer's care. These options will need to be evaluated and researched for the quality of care and safety they will provide.

When choosing a facility, include in your discussion how long your loved one will be able to remain there, especially as the disease progresses. Some facilities will provide care only until a certain stage of the disease, and then you will be looking again for placement. The least amount of moves your loved one will have to go through will be best for them, as well as for you. Alzheimer patients do not always take well to change. It is scary to them and they may feel as if they have been abandoned. It will take time for them to adapt to new surroundings. So, look for a place that is a home away from home, so that he/she can remain in that facility without intermittent moves. At this point, I encourage you to seek added support and/or counseling for yourself. It is not easy to leave your loved one.

The signs and symptoms that your loved one presents with will have a huge impact on the facility you choose. Decisions are difficult. Whatever decision you make, will be the best it can be. If you end up changing your mind as time passes by, so be it. This is normal, it is expected, and it is OK. Sometimes, it is hard to know what will work for you or your loved one until you have actually gone through it.

Please note: When choosing a facility away from home, really examine the daily activities of the caregivers and the other patients, as well as the environment they are living in. Is it clean? Does it look well kept? Does it have an odor? Do the patients look clean and are they presentably dressed? Does everyone appear to be in a good mood or happy?...or do they look stressed and upset? Are the caregivers attentive to the patient's needs? Is it a locked facility? Many facilities say they are adequately staffed and trained for the care of patients with Alzheimer's, but that is far from the truth. You want your loved one to be cared for with love, compassion and an understanding of care required for someone with Alzheimer's disease. There are multitudes of caregivers that provide wonderful care to the elderly; but it takes a special trained person to care for someone with Alzheimer's.

I would also like to mention----there is a saying "don't judge a book by its cover". This is true for facilities, also. You can be in the most beautiful of care facilities and find out the care they provide is far from being what it should be. So, take your time choosing a facility... if you can. Kind of like what you do when buying a house.

CHAPTER 7

HOSPICE

I am an advocate for Hospice and should your loved one need the services they provide, I highly recommend them. The concept of hospice goes back hundreds of years ago. I have been told that it was primarily for the care and support of the person as a whole-- mind, soul and spirit. This evolved into the care for the sick and incurable. Today, it is very much the same. They provide care to those who have a life threatening, terminal illness. They address the physical, social, emotional and spiritual needs for the patient and the family, and they provide this care no matter where it is needed---in the home, nursing homes, care facilities, shelters, daycares or prisons.

If your loved one meets the criteria in accordance with hospice guidelines, arrangements can be made for hospice to come in and help with their care. Most Alzheimer's patients under hospice care are in the end stages. They present with a significant, steady decline, and/or have an additional terminal illness. Hospice is not only for the actively dying patient. A referral from your doctor will begin the process of extra care for your loved one. Throughout the country, there are multitudes of people under the care of hospice who have Alzheimer's/ Dementia. Hospice is there to support, inform and help the family, as well as provide care to the ill. The following are some of the services hospice provides:

-Social workers that can help with needed information, counseling, and support for your families' needs, as well as an array of other concerns

-Certified Nursing Assistants that provide personal care, such as bathing, hair washing, shaving, reading, walks outside, etc.

-Nurses to manage and administer medications, teach, inform, monitor and manage health conditions, as well as provide support.

-Chaplains who provide emotional and spiritual support whenever needed.

-Volunteers who spend additional personal time with the patient or help the family with get-away time.

-Medical Doctors that will oversee and manage patient care services such as symptoms, medications, treatments and orders for adjustable beds, wheelchairs and much more. With these professionals coming in regularly, you can be relieved of some of the concerns you may have, receive added support, and get some needed rest. Your loved one will get one-on-one care, and you can feel more comfortable knowing he/she is well taken care of during the final stages. As a matter of fact, the most repeated response I have heard from family members is, "I don't know what I would have done without hospice."

TIP—If there has been an early diagnosis of Alzheimer's/ Dementia and/or if symptoms have just begun, it may be to your pleasure to take some special time together with your loved one.

CHAPTER 8

TIME FOR THAT TRIP

Now may be the time to enjoy some things that you may not have done in the past while your loved one is still able. For instance, take that vacation that you planned for years ago, but never took. Do something you have always wanted to do, but never took the time to do it. This may be the only chance you have to share another part of your life together while you both can still enjoy it.

Prior to making these plans, it would be wise to discuss them with your doctor. If your loved one has not actually been diagnosed with Alzheimer's/Dementia, your trip to the doctor will probably include a blood work-up, a good patient history, (if he doesn't already have one), the performance of various cognitive function tests, as well as a general medical exam. These steps will help the doctor determine if the symptoms are related to Alzheimer's/Dementia or if they are caused by another underlying illness. Whatever the case may be, the doctor will be able to advise you if a vacation or trip would be prudent at that time.

This would be a good time to learn as much as you can about the disease process. Ask your doctor questions. It is important to know as many facts about this illness as you can. Having knowledge about the disease and being prepared with factual information could help you prevent some future distressing episodes with your loved one. There is so much you need to learn and be prepared for. There will be times that you become frustrated and exhausted. You may have times that you get angry, bitter or even resentful. You could say some things that you will feel guilty about and regret later. These situations are what I hope could be prevented or minimized…and they can be… through knowledge and preparation. So ask questions and share your concerns. Your doctor may even suggest attending a support group. At the back of this book, I have listed several resources available for information about Alzheimer's/Dementia. Some may change over time and will need to be updated. However, the Internet is another helpful tool for this information. Just type in ALZHEIMER'S or DEMENTIA and it will take you to sites full of information. Also, your local yellow pages can give you information about facilities and day cares available in your area for those with Alzheimer's/Dementia. Again, due to modern technology, yellow pages may soon become obsolete.

***SAM had been diagnosed with Alzheimer's for about three years now. He was pretty much oriented to his surroundings, his wife and his family, but would have his periods of forgetfulness…sometimes one worse than another. He was able to pretty much take care of himself, with a little extra help provided by his wife. He was able to toilet, feed, shower and dress himself. Sometimes he would dress himself not fit for the occasion, but when told, would simply go in and change his clothes. They were getting dressed to go out to dinner one night, and he looked fine except for putting on a pajama top, in place of a shirt. When his wife graciously told him about his apparel, he quietly removed the pajama top and put on a nice shirt his wife had chosen for him. The dinner was a success.

A short time later, his wife figured she would take advantage of his alertness while she could, and decided it was time to travel and visit family up north. She had spoken to Sam's doctor, and he agreed that now was a good time to take this trip, instead of putting it off too long.

Prior to arriving at their destination, there were some minor episodes that caused her to wonder if it was a good idea to continue on their way. For instance, Sam had grabbed the steering wheel from her while driving on the interstate parkway. She could not figure out what made him do it, but was thankful the situation did not become a major ordeal. Also, during the entire trip, she said his favorite statements were, "When are we going to be there?" or, "How much longer?" She reminisced about the times of stopping to use the restroom. When she had to go, she would pull over and encourage Sam to use the restroom also. However, he would always say, "I don't have to go." Yet, when they got back on the road, he would say, "I have to go to the bathroom."

Then there were the awkward moments of which restroom she was going to use for Sam. She was not sure if he could go safely go into the men's bathroom by himself, or if it was better to take him into the women's restroom. She played it by ear with each of her stops. Some places had male/female restrooms, which seemed to work out the best, and when that was not the accommodation, she took him into the female restroom, into her stall, and that worked out fine also. With some minor explanations to those around her, she found out that most people were very understanding and it was not as big of an ordeal that she thought it would be. She also learned to "make light" of the situation and found that laughter was also good medicine. It eased her concerns and others. She actually met some people that had relatives with Alzheimer's and they shared similar stories.

She learned that Sam did not always want to get in the car when she wanted him to get in—nor did he always understand "how" to get in the car. She knew she could not leave him alone in the car when she would have to pay for something, as there was always the chance he could wander off. She was thankful for the drive-thru's and made use of them when she could. Otherwise, Sam went where she went.

All in all, the trip was wonderful. He enjoyed all of his family and they in turn, enjoyed him. She said she was so glad she had taken the trip when she did, and putting up with those minor mishaps was just another way of learning to cope with what was to be expected. She said she would not have traded it for anything.

"Love is patient, love is kind." 1 Cor.13:4 NIV

Part III

THE PROGRESSION OF ALZHEIMER'S

There is a basic, progressive decline with Alzheimer's disease. The following will give you a "general" idea of its pattern. Please keep in mind that each person may not present with symptoms in the exact same order or manner, although most will be very similar. Some signs and symptoms may appear at the same time. I have listed the symptoms only as a guide to the disease progression, and have followed with a more detailed explanation of each.

--forgetfulness/confusion/wandering

--behavior changes-loss for words

--weight loss

--change in sleep habits

--loss of control with bowel and bladder

--changes in speech and word pronunciation-word salad

--gait disturbances-inability to walk-falls

--change in eating habits

CHAPTER 9

CONFUSION/FORGETFULNESS

At first, they will begin to forget little things. They may not be able to find the word they are thinking about or will be unable to express the word that is "on the tip of their tongue." As the forgetfulness progresses they could forget where they put things, forget a name, or as with Harry, forget their way back home. These episodes may happen only on occasion and may be overlooked by family members as sheer, simple forgetting. However, with more repeated episodes, at more frequent intervals, attention will be drawn to the concern of their actions. Someone once told me that he "never saw it coming" with his wife. It kind of just "sneaks up on you."

***SAMUEL was eating dinner with his family. He was asking someone to pass the potatoes, but could not remember the word ---potato. "Pass me the _____. Could you hand me the _____, the _____." Unable to remember the word "potatoes", he finally said, "Hand those over there to me," and pointed to the potatoes.

NOTE: Sometimes if a word does not quickly come to their mind, if we wait a little and not focus on their inability to remember a word, it may come to them. Or, if we suggest the word for them, it "eases" the unrest. Ex: "Do you want the potatoes?".

During some conversations they may not be able to understand everything that is being said. They may ask you to repeat that again, or say, "What did you say?" or they may look at you with a gazed look on their face. There may be times they have difficulty speaking, and silly sentences or words will be said in place of normal ones. Some will laugh at themselves or ignore it. Others will feel angry because they realize their error, but are unable to recognize why the error occurred or how come they could not stop it. They may forget they did something, such as going to the store. Some will ask their spouse, "When are we going to the store?" The spouse may respond with the fact that they already went to the store and the discussion could end right there. However, there are those that will come back ten minutes later and ask again, "When are we going to the store?" If the situation becomes redundant and monotonous for the spouse, it may be effective to tell them, "The store is closed today, but we will go tomorrow", or "We will be going later on after dinner", or "We are not going right now, but why don't we go for a walk?" or…. something similar to that nature. Most will accept this solution or redirection and forget to ask later on. The objective is to ease their mind. When they feel comfortable with the answer given them, they are much more relaxed and at ease. When they feel 'at ease', you, also, will be 'at ease'.

***ARTHUR was sitting quietly on the sofa looking at the activity going on in another room. I walked up to greet him. "Good afternoon, Arthur. How are you today?" "I'm good," he replied with a smile on his face. "When are we going to eat? I haven't eaten in a long time. They don't feed you around here." I replied, "Arthur, I know it may seem like a long time, but you already ate your lunch." He thought for a moment and said,

"Oh, I did? What did I have?" I replied, "Yes, you did Arthur. You had a big plate of spaghetti with a couple of pieces of garlic bread." He stopped and thought some more, and then happily responded, "I love spaghetti. I must have really enjoyed it!"

TIP—there are others that may not be convinced as easily. They may get adamant and continue to say they have not eaten. Sometimes the best thing to do is bring them something to eat, perhaps a snack or something little. That may solve their unbelief and hunger. Please keep in mind, because their brain is not functioning correctly, even though they have eaten, they truly think they are hungry at that moment. However, in some cases, if a patient previously had a poor appetite and suddenly began eating again, he/she may truly be hungry. You will know if your loved one needs to eat or not. He/she just may really be hungry.

***JANICE would leave the same time every day for work. Even though Tom, her husband, was retired, he would get up every morning with her and they would start the day by eating breakfast together. The routine was the same this particular morning. Tom kissed Janice goodbye, and out the door she went. About two hours after she had left, Tom heard the front door open. It was Janice. She was calm, but very quiet, and had a disturbed look in her eyes. With concern, Tom asked her what she was doing home at this time of day. Not responding to his question, she walked over to the sofa and just sat there, staring at the wall. With more concern, he asked her again why she was home so early. He said, "She looked at me as if she was lost." She finally said, "I can't remember how to get to work. I have been driving around thinking it would come to me, but I just can't remember." Tom said, "Until that moment, I had never suspected a problem. She had never shown any other symptom until that day."

CHAPTER 10

Progression..with Behavior/Cognitive Changes

Some people can get very bitter or angry when they realize something is changing in them, but can't figure out what it is. They may become aggressive, hit, scream fight, or become threatening. Some may use language they never used before. At this point, you need to be careful, because they usually cannot control why they are acting out in this manner. The potential for someone getting hurt is there. Their sense of realization to themselves, others, or even their surroundings, is slowly deteriorating. These periods of high anxiety, fearfulness, combativeness or even paranoia and hallucinations, could arise at any time and may need to be addressed. They could be for a short time, or they could continue indefinitely. The time period is different for each. Some may never experience one of these episodes. Seeking assist from your doctor may lead to medications and advice that could help alleviate some of these symptoms. However, if these occurrences continue or escalate, they may create an unpleasant atmosphere that will lead you to seek other alternatives.

Tip: Please be aware of all behavior changes that suddenly present themselves. These can also be clues to pain, anxiety, frustration or depression.

***GEORGE lived at home with his wife. They had been married almost 43 years, and he had been diagnosed with Alzheimer's approximately seven years ago. Up until this point, his wife had accepted their lifestyle change. She was dedicated to taking care of her husband and had done an excellent job. One day while sitting watching TV, George suddenly began complaining to her about "a woman" being in his home and he wanted her out right now. (The woman he was talking about was his wife.) At first, she tried to convince him there was no one else there. She soon realized he was talking TO her, ABOUT her. He remained adamant she was lying and insisted she leave. The more she corrected him and said she was his wife, the angrier he became. It was getting to the point that his fist was clenched and he demanded she remove herself from the premises. At one point he told her she resembled his wife, but insisted that she was dressing like his wife so she could trick him into thinking it was his wife. She finally realized it was unsafe to remain in his presence, so she went to a neighbor's house for a short time. This was the first time she had ever become frightened by his actions. When she returned home about thirty minutes later, he welcomed her with a hug and told her about the woman that was in their home who would not leave. There were similar episodes like this for the next few months. A trip to the doctor's office, a change in medication, and the passing of some time, alleviated these occurrences.

***CHARLIE was scooting himself all over in a wheel chair. Although he could not stand, he was able to scoot himself in his wheelchair by using his legs and feet. For some reason, on this particular day, he became aggravated with a closed closet door. He began cussing, swinging his arms, banging on the door and kicking it with his feet. Not knowing what he wanted or what was bothering him made it even more difficult to settle him down. The door was opened for him so he could see inside, to no avail, and then closed again. Neither of these two actions would ease the aggravation Charlie was feeling. He was seeing something that we were not seeing. He was finally wheeled to another area. Even though he was out-of-sight of the closet, it took him at least 5 minutes before he calmed down. Five minutes can seem like forever when someone is agitated and cannot be consoled. Although redirection, by moving him to another area, helped in this situation, it may not always be the case. Helping your loved one through a frustrating episode could result in chaos. Getting Charlie away from the closet without harm to him or anyone else was not an easy task.

With the progression of the disease, I believe there comes a time that the patient begins to realize that a change is taking place in their brain. This is, in its own way, traumatic to them because they know it is not a good change…and it cannot be controlled by them.

Like Martha, they feel it… know it…. but have difficulty describing it. I believe it is not painful physically, but it can be emotionally and mentally. This, to me, is one of the hardest and saddest times of dealing with this dreaded disease.

***CONNIE would walk around the facility daily. She was in an earlier stage of Alzheimer's and to look at her or talk to her briefly, you would have never known she had Alzheimer's. She was a delightful, pleasant lady. However, on several occasions I would find her sitting on the edge of a couch, crying. I would sit alongside her and ask her what the matter was or ask if I could help her in any way. She would look at me, crying, and say, "My head doesn't feel right. Something is wrong, I know it is," or say, "I don't like what is happening to me." Trying to comfort her, I would put my arms around her and hug her. Sometimes I would tell her this would soon pass, or I would try to change the subject by asking her to come walk with me for a while. This would ease her mental anguish and help her get her mind off what she was thinking. Other times I would get her a cup of tea and sit with her. Something, anything, to just help her forget what she was thinking. Telling her it was going to be all right didn't seem appropriate and usually did not help at all.

***CAMERON on the other hand would act pretty much in the same manner, except, at times, she would come up to me and say, "I'm not crazy, they are… but I feel like I am." And then there were times that she would say, "Take this feeling away. I don't like it!"- as she held her hands tightly to the sides of her head.

***LOUISE would have periods of crying spells – for no recognized reason – except, she knew there were changes taking place. At times when she would speak coherently, she would say that it upset her inside to be unable to express her feelings, or "to get the words out". She would want to say something, but the words would not come. This was very upsetting and sad…for her, as well as for the staff that was taking care of her. We would try to comfort her, to no avail. Finally, with repeated distraction and persistence in trying to change the subject or get her interested in something, she would forget her sadness… but only for a time. It would begin again later—sometimes 20 minutes later, other times hours or days later. This would continue, intermittently, until she had progressed to another stage.

You will want to help them, but you may not know how to. But--- you can be there for them. I have found that distracting their thoughts and changing the subject was most effective in many cases. Some people believe it is better to try and explain to them what is happening. Others say it is a waste of time to explain. I have found, in most cases, the more you try to explain to them what is going on, one of three things may happen: they feel worse: they become more upset: or they don't understand what you are explaining. After all, they have a hard enough time dealing with a changed feeling in their head, let alone trying to understand why or how? Not only that, those who actually know they have this disease are already tormented by the fact that they have it. As time goes by, when you are faced with those moments, you will find out what works best for you and your loved one. Sadly to say, there is not always a simple remedy.

Many times it has been effective to use music therapy. Music can change a behavior or a feeling. It relaxes, calms and creates a soothing atmosphere. Many will recognize "old time" favorites. Some will prefer other types of music that you thought your loved one would have never cared for. Experiment with music and maybe even try to dance with your loved one---sing a song or hum. You may be surprised.

One family member told me that the hardest part for her was when she truly recognized THERE WAS A PROBLEM. She said that one day her husband looked at her with the phone in his hand, with a sad, but serious perplexed look on his face and said, "I don't know what to do with this."

"Then you will call upon Me and come and pray to Me, and I will listen to you." Jer. 29:12 NIV

TIP: Sometimes medications can help with these feelings. With correct dosing and monitoring, they just might be able to ease that uncomfortable feeling. However, medications are not always the answer. Consulting the doctor is encouraged if periods like these persist.

In time, they will forget family names and people who are close to them. When they do recognize someone close, they may not show affection, or may act disinterested. If they are in a facility, and the family visits, the Alzheimer's patient may not show excitement when their visitor arrives or show disappointment when their visitor leaves. They may even become "attached" to another Alzheimer's patient in the facility, and think that he/she is their spouse. To family members and friends, this will be disheartening. With situations like this, please remember, they do not know what they are doing. They really believe in their head, at that time, the person IS a loved one. Sometimes a gentle persuasion to remove your loved one from the vision of the other patient will "re-direct" their thoughts and they will again focus--as they do--on their visit with you. There may be times that your loved one may not recognize you as their spouse, but, at the same time, is very comfortable around you----still knowing that something about you is very familiar and comforting. Its ok to get some enjoyment from the fact that they still find you comforting to them. These are difficult times for the family. It is a lot easier to say "accept this" than it is to "accept this". My thoughts and prayers be with you at these difficult times.

***SAM'S family would visit him several times a week. Sometimes his family would leave disappointed because he did not recognize them during their visit, or respond to them the way he usually would. However, many times after the family left, Sam would sit quietly for a while and all of a sudden say, "My wife was here", or "My wife saw me today." There were other times that I would go up to him after they had left and say, "I saw you sitting with your family." He would respond with, "That was my daughter," or "It's nice they came," or, "Were they here?" with a slight smile on his face, even though during the visit, he did not know who they were. So, for all of you out there, don't think that your visits are wasted or you are not recognized. Some part of that visit may be remembered in their mind and recollected later. For those patients who do not speak…facial expressions say a lot. Eye contact, hand holding, touch, just being there means a lot. And don't think for one minute that a person who has no smile or no expression of happiness on their face means they are not happy to see you. The brain controls all of our responses. The damage to the brain could be in the area that gives the expressions. Therefore, their ability to give a loving smile, or a twinkle in their eye, or a happy "hello" look just may not be there "at that time". Often, it is so much harder on the family than it is on your loved one. With knowledge and understanding of this disease, it could make it a little easier for both of you.

***MARIE loved music, therefore, we would play it quite often. It seemed relaxing and calming not only to her, but to many of the patients. Marie was a beautiful lady. She was a famous dancer in her time, and had danced for people all over the world. I was told, "It was her life." She spoke very little, but when she did speak, it always included the phrase "I love to dance!" When I talked to her about dancing, she had a look in her eyes of pure delight, as well as a glow on her face that you wished you could have captured and framed. Her memory held lots of phrases on how much she loved to dance, and sometimes the music helped those phrases and thoughts come to the surface.

I look at it this way. The brain is made up of millions of nerve cells. These nerve cells hold our thoughts, words, phrases, actions, feelings, etc., and they transmit all these things from one cell to another, down a pathway. Normally, as we need the words, actions or thoughts, the nerve cells miraculously send the information from one cell to another and out they come. In an Alzheimer's patient, their cells are being destroyed bit by bit. So, as the cells are destroyed, so are the words, thoughts, actions, phrases, etc. But, because some of these things are kept in so many of the cells, they all can't be destroyed at the same time. As time goes by, they may take a little longer to "get out" because of the damage to the cells along the pathway, or they may come out as an incomplete word, incomplete phrase, incomplete memory, or what we might call "word salad"...... mixed up verbiage that we have a hard time trying to understand. So, when least expected, something normal could be expressed.

TIP: I have had many patients that cannot, or will not speak a clear word for long periods of time, that suddenly come to me and say, "You work hard", or ,"Your tired," or "..lots of writing." They watch you and DO notice things when you least expect it. Never underestimate what they may do or say.

Let's take the thought....WE GO TO MY MOMS HOUSE TO EAT TURKEY. THE TURKEY WAS ALWAYS TENDER AND JUICY. Verbally, it could come out something like this..."Tender turkey we eat" or like this... "It's a juicy dinner for turkey" or "Moms to eat turkey now". Later on in the disease process-- as more cells get destroyed-- not only are words mixed up, but letters and words are missing or put in the wrong place. For instance, it could come out similar to... "smurkey, smurkey, smurkey teat with mom", or "jouse to go dimmmmmmkey" or "turkey was mender and huicy."

The type of work a person has done in their past has a huge impact on what is said. One gentleman was involved in fishing most of his life and would often say two or three phrases related to his boating experiences. He would repeat these over and over again. Another gentlemen was in the army and often spoke, as best he could, with words related to experiences he had there. Another was a bookkeeper who repeated numbers for a long time. Some will repeat names of people you don't know, but when you tell a family member what name was said, they will say, "That's his sister!", or, "That's his aunts husband," or "He's reminiscing about a favorite television show he always watched and that was his favorite person in that show."

Things they have done in their past may also create a physical reaction. For example, a patient who was an office manager in her past would walk around giving pertinent instructions to her fellow co-workers. The instructions were actually being given to her caregivers. Sometimes she would get anxious and distressed because she felt things were not getting done on time or in the proper manner and she had deadlines to meet. Another example was when a past- employed law enforcement officer would suddenly be on the lookout for violators of the law. The violators would actually be the ones that were taking care of him. In his head, he had to protect, and they were the perpetrators. His protective responses were sometimes aggressive. Keeping him assured that a particular situation was under control, removing the "perpetrator" from the room, using re-direction techniques, such as leading him away from the immediate area and/or offering a drink or food item, while maintaining a calm demeanor, were some important management tools in caring for unexpected situations that would arise. Most of the time, occurrences can be handled. Yet, there are other times that an intervention may be warranted.

***LORETTA was sitting at the table waiting for lunch. I asked her how she was doing. "Just fine, thank you," she said. I then asked her if she was hungry. She said, "Yes, I am. I am just waiting for the—(hesitating)—the show to begin, and things get going."---meaning—she was waiting for lunch and was hoping it would hurry up and get there—or—she had a history of dining while a show was going on and she believed she was right there. Whichever it was, she was lady-like and at the same time, so cute the way she said it. Even though the brain could not put her words or thoughts in the proper perspective, she understood what she meant. I assured her lunch would be served shortly, and she was very thankful.

***LIZBETH was having difficulty finding her room. "I can't find my room. Someone took it out of here." she said. I assured her that someone brought it back, that it was down the hall and I offered to take her to it. We walked down the hall and her picture was on the door. This showed her it was her room. She looked at the picture of herself and knew right away it was hers. However, she was not pleased with how much older the picture looked compared to what she remembered of herself. "That looks like me. Why does it look so old?" I told her it was a beautiful picture, but if she wasn't pleased with it, we could take another picture later. I have also said, "It must have been a bad day when that picture was taken." She had agreed on both accounts and would walk into her room. (Her room was where she was most comfortable. You may find a special area in your home that seems to be more comforting for your loved one.) She would then ask, "Does this cost anything? If it does, I don't want it." I assured her she had nothing to worry about with the cost of the room, food or anything, that it was all taken care of and it was hers. She was so pleased and thankful that someone had provided this for her. Fifteen minutes later, Lizbeth was in the hall looking for her room, again.

They will continue to disorganize their sentence structure or thoughts. Earlier they could speak a normal sentence –with perhaps some silly word here and there. But now, other words are replacing the correct words more frequently. EX: "I want to serva that slink," or, "Can I prespect my own derpa?"

At this stage, I believe they hear you and understand you to a certain degree, but being able to express themselves correctly, all the time, gradually becomes more difficult for them, and, of course, more frustrating for the family. With this loss for words may come anger, sadness, depression or emotional pain –for the patient as well as the family. Some may stop and pause for a moment to try and absorb what you said. They don't pick up on things as quickly as we do. Their brain needs to try and process what has been said to them, and they too, may realize they are having a problem.

TIP—Try to give them time to express their feelings and/or to try and get their thoughts composed as best as they can. You may sit there a few minutes or so, but waiting to give them that chance to respond to your question or statement may be worth your while. You could even repeat your statement to them to refresh the thought, or you could repeat it with different words. Ex: "Let's go for a walk" - changed to- "Come walk with me."

Sooner or later, they will lack the ability to realize they have a loss for words. At that time, most of the anger, sadness or depression they once had, will be gone. At least it appears to be that way. I say this because, as time goes by, they less frequently show signs or symptoms of those emotions. They become totally engulfed in their "own little world".

NOTE: There are some that will develop seizure activity. They may stare at something for a long period of time, and not blink or move their eyes to the left or the right. When the staring stops, and they can make eye contact again, they may want, or need, time to sleep for several hours. This is usually ok. Some may present with grand mal seizures, where they shake around violently in bed or in their chair. This could last for several seconds or minutes. Call 911 and follow the operator's instructions. Until help arrives, if they are in a chair, support them to prevent them from falling out and causing injury. If they are on the floor, remove surrounding objects that can be of harm to them, place a pillow under their head, and try your best to remain calm. A gentle touch of your hand on them and a soft reassuring voice is helpful. If they are bleeding, apply pressure to the bleeding area and wait for help. I have had many patients that presented with seizure activity. They were usually placed on anti-seizure medication to help prevent further seizures from happening. Although a seizure can be frightening and is not pleasant to see, I have never seen (and hope I don't) a patient's life end because of it.

CHAPTER 11

Progression...with Toileting

They may begin, or have already begun to become incontinent ---that is-- accidentally wet or have a bowel movement in their pants. Some will have no idea their pants are soiled, some will tell you they are wet, (or at least try to tell you) and others may try to remove the soiled clothing themselves privately in the bathroom. And, of course, there are those that will refuse to let you change them at all. Depending upon the advancement of the disease, the patient, and/or your response to this situation, will determine your outcome of dealing with this matter. Incontinence can be very humiliating to them, at first. Care in this matter is essential for maintaining their dignity, especially earlier in the disease when they actually realize they have soiled their pants.

TIP-- Whether your loved one walks or is chair-bound, you may find that if taken to the toilet several times a day around the same time every day, they will become accustomed to this "training" and urinate or have a bowel movement in the toilet and not in their pants. This can be helpful to you, in earlier stages, and can help them maintain their dignity as long as possible.

If "training" is not possible, incontinence pull-up diapers can be purchased at your local supermarket or pharmacy. They are an "enhanced" type of underwear that prevent leakage onto clothing if someone were to have an accident in their pants. They are similar to a diaper, but designed for an adult. Either way-- toileting or pull-ups—can be a lot less work for the caregiver.

***ELLA was found in her bathroom, talking to herself and trying to clean herself up. She was troubled and distressed. I asked her if she could use my help. She looked at me with troubled eyes and said, "Something is stuck, it needs to come down, and I can't get it. Help me." She was dealing with a case of constipation and was trying to tell me the best way she could. Constipation seems to be prevalent in many Alzheimer's patients. "Our" normal response to the feeling of a bowel movement is to push. Alzheimer's patients will get to the stage that they do not feel the urge to push, know how to "push", or even know what it means to "push". Therefore, the stool remains in the rectum and the patient will become constipated. It would be wise to be very much aware of this symptom. If you notice a change in bowel habits, you may want to contact your doctor. Early awareness can prevent "impaction"—which is a severe case of constipation that may require a doctor's intervention-- or even surgery. There are many over-the-counter medications available to prevent constipation, as well as those prescribed by your doctor.

***JEFF was in the bathroom when I entered his room. I asked if everything was ok and he responded with, "Yes". I waited and he did not come out. I asked if I could come in. He replied with "Yes"- again. Opening the door, I saw Jeff with stool all over the floor, on his clothing and on the wall. I said, "Here, let me help you with this. It looks like you are having a bit of a hard time." He let me help him, but he also helped "me" clean up the mess by pulling toilet paper and paper towels off the rolls and handing them to me—yard after yard of toilet paper. I was thankful, I let him know I was, and he was pleased he could help.

> TIP-- A gentle response to a "sticky" situation helps to maintain a calm behavior as well as a patient's dignity. You will feel better, also…after everything is cleaned up.

***KAREN was incontinent at times. Usually, if she was taken regularly to the toilet, she remained unsoiled. One day she began to remove her clothing in the living area. She would start by tugging at her blouse and get it half way off, only to be assisted with putting it back on. Then she would begin removing her pants—pulling at the waistband, pulling at the legs and becoming restless. After several episodes of this behavior, I finally suggested that she be taken to the toilet. WHA-LA – that was the answer. It was her way of telling us that she was uncomfortable and had to use the toilet now. We learned that when we saw her trying to remove clothing, it was time to take her to the bathroom. This was one problem that was resolved.

***MARK would sit quietly in his wheel chair. He spoke very few words. He would usually sit there and fall asleep or just watch others with their daily activity. Mark spoke very few words and he was toileted on a regular schedule. This particular day he became very restless, and anxious. He started scooting himself around the living room area with his feet, shaking his hands. "Help me, Help me", he would say. I would try to talk to him and find out what the matter was, to no avail. He continued this behavior for about ten minutes, and his anxiety increased. I finally asked someone to assist me and we took him to the toilet. Instead of saying "Help me, help me," he was now saying, "Thank you, Thank you." He had to use the toilet. Although taking him to the toilet alleviated his request for help several times, it did not solve the problem 100% of the time. There were other times that toileting did not ease his anxiety. To this day I will never know the reason for some of those high anxiety periods. Even though some of them did not last for long periods of time, it always concerned me that I couldn't help determine what his uneasiness was attributed to. I was thankful, though, that there was prescribed medication that could be used at those times to help lower those episodes of anxiety.

> TIP: Alzheimer's patients can develop urinary tract infections easily. Some may not drink as much fluids as they use to, which can cause them to become dehydrated, which can lead to urinary infections. Watch for behavior changes, increased confusion, strong odor to urine, fevers and changes in urine color. Consult with your doctor if any of these symptoms occur and persist. Hydration is of the utmost. Fluids, fluids, fluids!!! Many times they won't ask for a drink. You will need to offer regularly.

Just another little note, if not already mentioned: there may be times that your loved one will refuse to sit on the toilet. No matter how hard you try to convince them it is time to go to the bathroom, they absolutely will not sit down on the toilet. They could keep trying to prevent you from pulling their pants down, and/or will not bend their knees to sit. This can become frustrating. They really are not sure what you are trying to do, or…they just don't want to go. Try talking to them in a calm manner. Perhaps you can change the subject while talking and distract them from what you are trying to do..("here, let me do this", or, "let me help you," or "could you hold this for me?", or, "do you know what I saw today?"…at the same time you are gently trying to lower them to sit on the toilet. Once they are sitting, keep talking to them. If this fails, it may be better to avoid using the toilet at that time and try again later.

CHAPTER 12

Progression.....with Safety Issues and More

Their balance and coordination will change, and with that change, decline will be noticed. They may start with walking slower at first, or hanging on to things that are near them as they walk. This gives them a more secure feeling. Of course there are those that cannot sense their feeling of "lack of balance". They can, and will, fall forward or backward without a sign. At first, there may be a noticeable unsteadiness when trying to get up or when they are bending over. They may look like they are going to fall, but are able to catch themselves and regain their balance. It is important to watch for these signs. If you see changes like these, alternatives (as discussed below) may be needed to prevent them from falling.

For the most part, almost all Alzheimer's patients have falls –at least once. Many times, after repeated falls, some will be afraid to get up and walk again. They may become very anxious with any attempt to transfer them from a chair to a bed or other position –for fear of falling. Some may resist your helping to move them and yell out or grab and hold on to whatever they can. Positive reinforcement and calm reassurance are important in assisting their transfer from a chair to a bed or wheelchair.

Others will just keep on trying to get up, forgetting they have fallen. As the disease progresses, they will not understand what a fall is or how to protect themselves against a fall. "Our" natural instinct is to grab something or brace ourselves for the fall with our arm or hand. They lose that instinct and fall without any thought to protect or brace themselves. The unsteadiness in walking will continue until they are unable to walk without assistance, or until a caregiver uses other measures to prevent the falls.

In a facility, with nursing supervision, usually a nurse will recognize the need for alternative measures prior to a fall, or at least after one fall. Wheelchairs can be ordered for those who are willing to remain in them. Some may need anti-tippers. These are metal devices on the back of a wheel chair that if the patient tries to lean backward, these metal forks will help prevent the wheel chair from tipping over backwards. The patient is still free to scoot around with his/her feet, anywhere he/she pleases, but remains safer. Many will learn to move their feet back and forth and propel the rolling of the wheelchair. The majority of patients sit quite comfortably in their wheelchair and actually seem to enjoy the freedom of scooting around. They should regularly be assisted out of the wheelchair to be toileted, or to bed for a nap, and/or be transferred to a recliner, chair or table. This gives them the opportunity to stretch their legs, helps in the prevention of sores on their buttocks (due to sitting too long), and breaks up the monotony of being confined to one place all day long. Until they are "trained" to sit in a wheelchair, on a sofa, or in a recliner without getting up, they will need constant supervision and someone to walk with them at all times.

Other items that are available to help prevent falls are as follows: <u>pommel cushions</u> (a saddle like cushion that sits in a wheelchair or a recliner that helps prevent a patient from sliding out); <u>geriatric chairs</u> (similar to recliners only with wheels for moving); <u>wedges</u> (cushions that are very thick at one end and gradually slope to a thinner thickness at the other end); <u>side rails on beds</u> (a patient can grab to help with assist out of bed); <u>bed or chair alarms</u> (alarms that will "sound off" if the patient is trying to get up; <u>canes and walkers</u>, etc. Sometimes the use of a physical therapist (depending upon the "stage" of Alzheimer's) can be of benefit in teaching the patient techniques for transferring (moving from one item to another) or walking. They can also offer professional advice on other safety alternatives.

TIP: There will come a time, as the disease progresses, that physical therapy for walking, standing, transfers, etc, will have no effect on your loved ones improvement. I believe, and have seen, that if the therapy continues, it will more than likely make your loved one frustrated, cost you money, or confuse your loved one into thinking they are able to walk, stand, or transfer and it will increase their potential for falls.

BRENDA was able to walk the entire facility. One day, while outside in a courtyard, she had fallen. The fall resulted in a fractured arm and a bruise to the forehead. She was unable to walk for several weeks after her injury. A cast was placed on the fractured arm, for which she did not understand this "hard, swootzel of a thing" that she carried around for many weeks. It was explained to her that she had a broken arm, but with little understanding and much forgetfulness. Fortunately, she never remembered the incident, was in no pain, and the cast became a part of her. Four weeks later she was up walking again, unsteady at times. Two months later, after several falls, she became wheelchair bound, and was very content.

***TIMOTHY was able to walk without difficulty for quite some time, until he began showing signs of decline. He began by walking much slower, grabbing furniture and holding on to help himself get up. Many times when he walked he would look down and stop to touch something he thought he saw on the floor. He would stay close to walls just in case he lost his balance. Most of the time he was fine walking, but the minute he started to bend over to pick something up, he would loose his balance and fall forward. One day he saw a box sitting on the floor and was curious about the piece of tape that was hanging from it. He kept trying to move the tape with his foot to no avail. He finally bent over to swing at the tape with his hand, lost his balance and fell forward. Fortunately, he was not injured and the box was removed. Before too long, Timothy required the use of a wheelchair and recliner. His "chair of choice" was the recliner. He was most comfortable there. However, there were times that he would try to get up, and being unable to walk anymore, had to be monitored judiciously for his own safety. A chair alarm was used to alert anyone if he tried to get out of his wheelchair. This device hung on the back of the wheelchair and was connected to his shirt by a clip. Each time he leaned forward, the clip would trigger the alarm to go off, which alerted the staff. The noise would usually startle Tim and he would stop and sit back in the chair. It prevented many falls, as well as kept the staff on their toes.

NOTE: Laws have changed over the years. There was a time that we could place a safety belt in a wheelchair, loosely around the patient's waist. When they would attempt to get up, they could go only so far, feel pressure at their waist, and this would alert them that they could go no further and they would sit back. However some laws consider this a restraint. I suggest for those in a facility to check with your current laws prior to the use of a safety belt. I might add, in partial defense of those law changes, they were done to protect the patients. There were, and still are, those that neglect patients by strapping them into wheelchairs and leaving them there all day.

Around this time, some patients may only be able to speak about 4 or 5 sensible words in a row. Most may say only 2 or 3 words that are understandable, similar to Brenda's description of her cast. I have noticed that during this phase, just someone sitting by these patients and letting them "talk" while you listen, keeps them more content than anything I have seen. They usually love company. It's like they genuinely enjoy someone just being there beside them. Patience to let them try and express what they are saying is encouraged, as well as support, love and understanding.

They may or may not be interested in looking at a book. If they are interested in it, they may just turn the pages and stare at some things along the way. I have seen many patients turn to one page and just look at that one page for hours, never delineating from it. Most all Alzheimer's patients will love to go for a walk, whether it is actually walking side by side with them, or if they are unable to walk, pushing them in a wheelchair…..especially around this time. They may chatter with word salad, or they may just walk and not say a single word. Being a good listener is imperative, as well as just being there with them. You "may" even hear a good, complete sentence that really makes sense, when you least expect it. Then you will know what's really on their mind at that moment. It is actually fun to walk with them and listen, and when you talk back to them, sometimes they actually act like they know what you are saying.

Who knows?? Maybe they do. And if they don't, just listening to them and spending the time with them can be enjoyable as well as rewarding.

TIP: In regards to falls, and helping a loved one to remain safely seated, I have found that giving them a baby doll to hold (and care for) puts them at ease. I have assisted several patients to a sofa to sit, given them a doll to hold an asked them to take care of it and watch it…. and they never moved from the sofa or tried to get up and walk. They were too busy caring for that "baby". (see…some things remain in some minds forever.) Of course, this can all depend upon the patient and their stage of Alzheimer's.

CHAPTER 13

Progression....with Sleep Changes

Y ou will begin to notice that their sleeping habits have changed. Most will sleep more as the disease progresses. They may fall asleep several times during the day while sitting in a chair. If you see this happening regularly, it will make the patient more comfortable if he/she were to be placed in bed for a nap every afternoon. Frequent checks to make sure they are asleep and safe in bed is always recommended.

> TIP --Take care in choosing the right chair for them to sit in. Sitting on a chair with no arms creates a potential for falling off the side onto the floor. The arm will act as a barrier and could prevent injury.

Some, on the other hand, will disregard their need for sleep. They will be up all hours of the night and day, until they are completely exhausted. When they finally "give out", they could sleep twenty-four hours or more without waking. If this were to happen, always take time for periodic checks to make sure they are sleeping restfully and comfortably and that there is not another problem occurring. If the periods of insomnia occur frequently, there are medications that can help decrease their wakeful times and help maintain a more scheduled sleep routine.

***JACKIE was pretty close to this stage. She was free to walk inside or outside in the fenced-in courtyard. She began falling asleep in the daytime with quick naps lasting 10-15 minutes long, at least 4-8 times a day. She had to be watched carefully, as sometimes she would fall asleep outside in the hot sun. Making sure they get plenty of fluids, if outside in the heat, is crucial to prevent dehydration.

One night, however, Jackie was unable to sleep. She was up all night, into everyone's room, drawer's, clothing, bathroom's, etc. She continued this into the next day, and the next night. She became totally exhausted, but slept no more than 10-30 minute intervals at a time. A mild sleeping pill was ordered, and she finally received the rest she needed.

TIP: With periods of increased sleep, movement to our muscles and circulation decreases. This becomes a higher risk problem for skin breakdown. If a person sits or lays in one spot consistently for long periods at a time, skin sores could easily develop. If you see the skin becoming red or purple or feels softer than normal, consider the length of time your loved one is sitting or lying on one spot. Consult a doctor if necessary prior to an open wound developing.

CHAPTER 14

Progression...with Appetite Changes

They will usually follow simple commands – sometimes reluctantly. They cannot be told to do more than one thing at a time. Most are still able to feed themselves. Some will use a fork or spoon, but will gradually revert to using their fingers only. The time will come when they need to be fed, or at least assisted to eat. Some may loose their appetite and will need to be encouraged to eat. One day you may sit down with them to eat and they will not want to. It may not be because they are not hungry, but because they do not recognize the food as food. They may not know what to do with it. Try to assist them with eating. You may have to offer the food on a spoon or fork and talk about something totally different than eating. If their attention can be focused on something else and you offer the food while doing that, they may take the first bite without concentrating and realize how good it does taste. Patience is so important with your loved one. It may take you an extra ten or fifteen minutes, but when they begin to eat that food or finally pick up the spoon themselves to eat, you will know the extra time spent was worth it. However, if they continue to refuse to eat, missing a meal or two will not hurt them. You can always offer it at the next meal, or give them something else later in the day. Sometimes they just do not want to eat. I have always learned that when they are ready to eat, they will eat. If I have done my best to offer them foods, and they still refuse, then they are not ready to eat.

There will be a few that do the complete opposite. They will want everything on their plate, and everything that is on someone else's plate. Some will grab whatever food they can, from whoever they can, while others will be content with their own plate. They all seem to want something in their mouth, and food seems to be the best thing. I have seen many that have picked up stones, bitten off pieces of styrofoam, paper, gloves, tissues, paper towels, and put them in their mouth and try to chew them. I have seen some that take the lids off of pop-top cans and put them in their mouth and chew them down to tiny pieces of metal. Keeping items such as these away from these patients is imperative. Never underestimate what they can, or will, do.

At some point, closer to end stage, some patients will automatically open their mouth to anything that gets near to their face, especially if they have declined to a point that they need to be fed by someone else. If they are still able to chew and swallow without difficulty, a regular diet can be maintained. However, as the disease progresses, they will have increased trouble with swallowing. They may choke, cough a lot during eating, begin to get a profuse runny nose during eating, or just move the food around in their mouth without swallowing. The diet can be changed from a regular diet to a chopped diet (cut up into very small pieces), to a soft diet (speaks for itself), or to a pureed diet (baby food like). You will be able to tell how well your loved one's swallowing habits are and regulate his/her diet accordingly. If you are not really sure of what to try, always go with the safest way. They may not like the change at first, but most will adapt in a very short time.

Nutritional supplements are also available to give your loved one the nutrients he/she may need if their eating habits have declined. There are also many types of home-made nutritional shakes that can be made. These may get the attention of your loved one, where regular food may not. You may want to discuss this with your doctor or someone who specializes in nutrition.

As their appetite decreases, they will lose weight. Please note that Alzheimer's patients will steadily lose weight over the period of their illness whether they eat or not, and each at certain intervals at a time. Some may have periods of slight weight gain, and then weight loss. This is part of the disease process and is expected. Again, brain cells are not functioning the way they should be. The brain controls all of our aspects related to nutrition and how food is used and metabolized in our body. With the brain not functioning correctly, the body does not utilize the nourishment from food correctly. Thus, weight loss takes place. Sometimes, certain medication regimes will help them sustain, or even gain some weight. However, with the normal progression of the disease, the weight loss will resume at some time in the future.

As the need for them to be fed by someone continues, the progression of the disease continues also. It will continue in this manner until the patient becomes weak, their appetite decreases, the diet changes to puree foods, choking episodes persist, and sooner or later, will end with his/her demise. There is no set time for the length of this process. Some Alzheimer's patients will die from other illnesses not related to Alzheimer's, and of course, those illnesses will have an effect on their quality and length of life. Each individual is different. Again, please remember, any one of the stages of Alzheimer's discussed could overlap one another, and a particular symptom may not always present itself exactly as explained. Any patient could "miss", and I use that word loosely, a certain part of the progression---which would be very rare, if at all possible. If they did, based upon my experiences, I would tend to believe that they had an underlying illness, they developed Alzheimer's at a very early age or at a very late age, or it was not Alzheimer's in the first place. With the way organism's, illnesses, medications, body systems, etc. change as time goes by, who is to say that Alzheimer's symptoms won't change to some degree?

Dear Friend: This is not an easy topic for me to touch upon, but I feel it should be mentioned. As with all of us, dying is inevitable. We don't really like to talk about it, but sooner or later, we will have to face this event. The progression of this disease, as is with most diseases, will take us to dying. With that, I would like you to know something. Almost every Alzheimer patient I have ever cared for has had a peaceful journey from this life. They did not suffer as some might think, and they had little or no pain. To me, this was a saving grace, especially after all the things the patient and family had already been through. My intention is not to make you look forward to the end, but to give you a little bit of hope knowing that most patients met their destination and end of life peacefully.

"Now faith is being sure of what we hope for and certain of what we do not see." Heb.11:1 NIV

PART IV

ESPRESSIONS OF OUR LOVED ONES

CHAPTER 15

DO THEY HAVE FEELINGS?

You might ask, "Do patients with Alzheimer's disease have feelings?" The answer is a definite ---YES, they do. However, they have a different response with feelings at the earlier stages of Alzheimer's, than they do during the later stages of the disease. In order to understand this topic, there are several questions we should contemplate.

Please read each one over twice and focus on the questions. It is important….. "Are they feeling like we would expect them to feel?"----- "Are they showing their feelings like we would show our feelings"-----"Do they react the same as we would?"

***SANDY rarely spoke. There were times that I wondered if she was ever going to speak again. She would sit, stare, eat, and nod on and off to sleep…once in a while she would mutter a gibberish type of speech. One day, there another patient (Bob) who was not having a good day. He was unreasonable and was yelling and complaining at everyone. No matter what you tried to do for him, he remained displeased. All of a sudden Sandy yelled, "Will you shut up!" She was annoyed by the actions of Bob, and she expressed her feelings. There have been many times when I was getting ready to leave and I would say, "I am leaving now, can I have a kiss goodbye?" Even though they were sitting there quietly, staring, or even walking around, peaceful-like in their own little world, many have turned their heads and given me a kiss on the cheek. All I had to do was take time to go to them and give them a kiss on the cheek, and they reciprocated. Yes, they have feelings.

***JIMMY would always sit without saying a word. His wife would come almost every day to feed him and join him for lunch. This one particular day he would not take his eyes off her. She would talk to him, without a response, and try to figure out why he was continually staring at her. She finally realized she was wearing a new pair of earrings that he was not familiar with. She asked him if it was the earrings he was looking at (she spoke to him all the time, even though he rarely responded, because she knew he understood more than what he portrayed to understand). To her surprise he responded with, "They're pretty." Not another word was said...... but he had noticed.

***STELLA was a little lady that loved to listen to music. She spoke only on occasion – basically when she felt like it. I brought a headset for her to listen to some music I thought she would enjoy. She loved it. She would sit there, fold her hands in front of her and just listen with her eyes closed. One day, after hearing the same songs, for several days, she said, "I'm tired of hearing that." She took off the headset and slammed it on the table. She was evidently bored with the same music day in and day out. Is that a feeling?

***I was talking to Katherine one day while doing one of my assessments. She sat there, not muttering a single word. Once in a while she would say a two to three word statement that made sense, but normally it was a gibberish type "conversation". I was brushing her hair, putting lotion on her legs and just talking to her, as I always did, not expecting any response. I said, "I just wonder what advice you would give to women on relationships and men." Suddenly, she said as clear as day, "Make sure he is worth the trouble." I laughed graciously, told her thank you for the advice, finished her care and packed up my things to leave. On my way out the door, she smiled and said something that was similar to, "Nice talk with girls. Do it again sometime." Imagine that!!!!!

***A member from a Catholic church would come by regularly and give Holy Communion. When the patients saw this person coming towards them, they would sit quietly and wait for their turn. Most knew why that person was there. After the words were said, and they took communion, some would make a sign of the cross.

***One man would walk around the facility all day long. If he saw a women getting ready to sit down at a table, and he was nearby, he would, in a gentleman-like manner, pull out her chair ever so gently, wait for her to sit down, scoot her in to the table, and proceed on his way.

***How about Michael who would sit with the Bible open in his lap. One day I picked up the Bible and said, "Would you like me to read something to you?" The only response was a grin. I took the bible, picked out some scripture and began to read. When I finished, He looked at me and said with a very slow stutter-like response, "Thank you. I couldn't have picked a better one." Please remember, this person normally did not speak full complete sensible sentences. As always, you never know when you will be amazed.

***A Christian song was played one day, for all to hear. Everyone was standing or sitting around in the living room. When the music started you could have heard a pin drop. There was no muttering, and very little movement, as they listened to the song. One man began to raise his arms above his head, as if praising God. He closed his eyes and moved his lips all the way through the song, with his arms held up. When it was over, he said quietly, "Thank you. Thank you so much." He got up and slowly shuffled away.

***LARRY was a very quiet man who spent most of his days sitting in a recliner looking out the window, watching others, or sleeping. He usually had very little to say and would respond with a 3-4 word brief statement, if anything at all. His wife would visit him regularly and they enjoyed meals together quite often. One day, through some mishap, his wife had an unexpected fall in front of him. She was safely assisted to the chair next to her husband. To her surprise, as well as all others who were present, her husband began to shed his tears and repeatedly say, "That's my wife. I love her. She is everything to me. I don't know what I would do without her." We were all in tears. We assured him she was OK as we took time to calm him. Finally a smile appeared and a gentle kiss to his wife.

***A pastor would come to the facility once a week. A group of patients were sitting around listening to him teach the Bible. There must have been about twenty patients sitting there listening. All their attention was on the pastor, and they knew to be quiet and listen. When the pastor was finished, he played "Amazing Grace". This is one of my favorite songs and it always makes me cry. Well, evidently it affects others in the same manner. You could look around the room and see how many had tears running down their faces. They knew, they felt, they loved, they remembered, but never spoke a word. They did not have to.

***There was a patient that would scoot herself in a wheelchair through the halls. On those occasional bad days, while she was scooting, she would make a noise as if crying. As I sat there watching, I could see the effect this woman had on the other patients. To my surprise, three other patients felt her sadness, or need, or whatever emotion was expressed, and each one of them, at different intervals, would get up from their chair, go to this woman in the wheel chair, and gently push her up and down the hall-- trying to alleviate her anxiety. Amazingly enough, the woman would relent from making the noise, as long as she was being pushed. When one got tired of pushing her, another one would get up and take his/her place. Not one ever spoke a word.

WARREN would enjoy his daily visits from his wife. She was very attentive to his needs. He would gently follow her through the halls as they walked together, and would chatter away in his unknown verbiage. She would hold his hand, and he would follow without question. They would sit together, side by side for hours, and then it would be time for her to leave. He sometimes would fall asleep on the chair, and not realize she left, and other times she would just leave and he would hardly notice. Yet, I can remember the countless times that once he was aware she was not there, he would come up to me with tears flowing down his face, and his lips quivering as he cried. He did everything he could to let me know he missed his wife, and she was gone. Gentle redirection, hugs and a walk arm in arm usually calmed this gentle man.

I have watched patients walk around a facility, almost all day long, with no stopping except to rest for five minutes or take time to eat. They are in their own "little world" wandering, walking, thinking. They may make a gesture of grabbing your arm as you walk by, (because they want you to walk with them) or they hold their arms out to you for a hug. They just want to be touched or recognized…just an acknowledgement of some kind. Some would be holding hands with another Alzheimer's patient, in a friendship-like manner. Others would sit down to rest and then gently put their hand on another individual's knee, or put their arm around another patient and just sit there. You could see the comfort, the closeness …..the feeling….that they shared. They may not have said anything, but they didn't have to. Their actions show they have feelings.

There are very few Alzheimer's patients that do not like to be hugged. Almost everyone I have met or had the opportunity to care for, has always appreciated and enjoyed a nice hug. It always seems to bring a smile to their face, and what's even nicer is that they reciprocate with a hug back. And another thing, there are two phrases that so many of these lovely people seem to remember. They will say them at unexpected times, and right up until the end of their life. Those two phrases are, THANK YOU and I LOVE YOU, TOO. No matter how disassembled their words are or how little they speak, given the opportunity and the right time, these words almost never fail to show up. And if they don't show up, just look into their eyes…you just might be able to understand that they do feel.

CHAPTER 16

DO THEY HAVE PAIN?

Yes, they do. But I believe, at least with most of them, it is not felt the same way that we feel pain. And again, it is dependent upon the stage they are in. It seems that a constant, nagging-like pain that we would feel, is felt with less intensity for them. Therefore, since they feel it less, they respond to it less. For the most part, they do not dwell upon the pain or complain about the pain like we do, and sometimes they can even be distracted from it… or so it seems. Their senses, evidently, do not relay the "feeling of pain" back to the brain in the same manner as it is done in our body. Our pain is felt because of the signals that are rapidly sent to our brain cells from the injury site. Remember, their brain cells are deteriorating, so the impulse of pain that is sent back to the brain either does not accept the "message" of pain, or it does not reach the receptor sites to let them know there is pain. Whatever the reason, it can be a blessing they do not feel pain as we do. I have seen many patients with very bad bruising and cuts on their faces, arms and feet (usually from falls). Usually, they forget what happened and say they have no pain, or they just make a few brief comments, such as, "That is sore there," and then go about their normal routine. When asked if they are in pain, they will usually say "No". Some may say, "Yes, a little", but act as if they have none. If one were to say, "No, I have no pain" and then walk away limping, holding their head or grabbing their arm, you know something is bothering them.

> TIP -- Sometimes rephrasing the question, "Do you have any pain?" to something like, "Are you hurting?", or "Does your arm hurt?", or "Does your head hurt?" may initiate a correct response.

Gently touching their arm and asking this question may get their attention and help them respond more appropriately, if they can. However, I have heard responses that have nothing to do with the question, so I encourage you to assess for other signs and symptoms, as follows.

***HEDDIE had multiple bruises and cuts from falling on the driveway into the bushes. There were several deep lacerations that needed to be cleaned and dressed regularly. When asked if she was in pain, she would say "No!" However, when it came time to take care of the wounds, she would bang her hand on the table three times very fast and say "OOOHHHHH"! It would take almost one hour to gently clean and put new dressings on her wounds. She would repeat this action two times at every dressing change, and that would be the end of her response. This would happen every time the dressing was changed...even up until the time the wounds were almost healed. Pain medication was always given prior to her dressing change.

Watching for signs and symptoms of pain can be a challenge for anyone. Sometimes it can make it difficult for even nurses and doctors to treat them. Watch for any changes in their attitude. If the way they act changes, it could be a sign something is bothering them. Perhaps they may frown, stop smiling, moan, furrow their eyebrows, or a simple, "Ouch!" Doctors and nurses will monitor blood pressure readings. If someone is having pain, usually the blood pressure will become elevated. However, with Alzheimer's patients, that is not always a reliable sign. Many blood pressures have been taken on Alzheimer's patients while they are sound asleep, resting comfortably and peacefully and some readings were astoundingly high. Yet, if they awaken, and a blood pressure is taken a few minutes later, it has completely returned to normal. I have no knowledge of why this happens, and it happens frequently. Perhaps whatever brain activity is going on while they are asleep creates a hyper excitability which raises the blood pressure. I don't know, but I am sure there is some physiological reason for this symptom.

Pain should also be considered when one responds with anger, aggressiveness, change in tone of voice, or restlessness. One patient I remember very well, could tolerate, what I, myself, thought would be uncomfortable. He had to have a specific procedure done at the doctor's office. During the procedure there was no change in the expression on his face, no moaning, no verbal or physical sign of discomfort. However, when the procedure was done and we were on our way out of the doctor's office, he said adamantly-- with a serious, angry look on his face, "I don't want there again anymore." He meant what he said.

***FRANKLIN was normally a quiet individual. He would sit in his chair, busy himself with watching other people and usually just keep to himself. He rarely spoke. However, if he did, it was very brief sentences, with some mixed up words in them. Sometimes you could understand what he was saying, and other times it was very difficult to interpret. Franklin did not like having a bowel movement in a diaper or a pull-up. He was use to being toileted, but did not always have a bowel movement when taken. At a time when he could verbalize and tell you he needed to go to the bathroom, there was no problem. But, as the disease progressed, he could not relay that information to you. He would have outbursts of aggressiveness and anger, and for the longest time, we could not understand the reason for his actions. He would pound his fists on the table, swing his arms at anyone that came near him, and rant and rave until he got someone's attention. When it was finally figured out that he was trying to let us know he needed to go to the bathroom, we would take him, he would have a bowel movement and the outburst would end. His trying to prevent himself from having a bowel movement in his pants created discomfort, the same way being constipated can be uncomfortable to us.

The stage of the disease plays an important part as to the response the patient will display if in pain. In the early stages, perhaps after recent diagnosis of the disease, he/she may display pain symptoms the same way you or I do. As the disease progresses, you may see different symptoms displayed when they are hurting. Keeping these things in your mind may help you to recognize when your loved one is troubled or in pain.

CHAPTER 17

DO THEY LAUGH?

Of course they do, but not as often as we would like, and sometimes not when we would expect them to. It all depends upon if they really thought something was funny, the stage of Alzheimer's, the timing, their condition, the mood they are in, or even if they understood what was said or what was happening. One day a co-worker told a joke and staff started laughing. After a few seconds had elapsed, a couple of the Alzheimer's patients also started laughing. Now, whether they understood the joke or were just laughing because we were, I could not tell you. But the more they laughed, the more we laughed and the more we laughed, the more they laughed. Then one of them said, "That was a good one!" It was great! They actually enjoyed laughing, and it had come naturally.

***JENNY loved to sing. One day I was trying to get her to sing with me, and for the others to join in. It was Christmas time, so I started singing some Christmas songs, hoping someone might remember, or at least, get some enjoyment from the song. Picture this…!!! I definitely cannot carry a tune. So here I am singing Jingle Bells, and I went off key... badly. I sounded totally ridiculous, and Jenny picked up on it. She laughed at me with a big hearty bellow and kept right on laughing. The more she laughed, the more everyone else laughed. She knew I couldn't sing and it must have sounded pretty darn funny to her, as well as the others... and a bit of embarrassment for me!

***IRENE will sit in her wheelchair most of the day and scoot herself all over the halls and through the living room. As she meanders through these areas, she will chatter away about work. Her most sincere "discussions" are related to the work she use to do. She talks to herself, or anyone that will listen, and so much enjoys sharing her past experiences. You may not totally understand what she is saying, but in her mind she is reliving those experiences and sharing them with you. All of a sudden she will begin to laugh. She has touched on something in her past that was funny to her. It is a beautiful thing to be there and see her enjoyment.

One of the funniest, most enjoyable moments I have seen is when a group of Alzheimer's patients were sitting watching a TV program. Now some may actually be able to "watch" the program and understand it, while others just sit and occasionally gaze at the TV or just look around the room. This program was playing a country song in the background and there were children, adults and older people doing a country line dance to the song. Someone on the program had messed up a few steps and fell, which made others bump into each other, which then created a domino effect and others began to fall. Almost every one of the patients began to laugh. The room was full of laughter. I just cannot explain how you feel when you see something like this. It may not be something you see often, but it does happen. By the way, no one was hurt on the program. They were laughing, too.

NOTE: Music was regularly scheduled at the facilities I worked in. A musician would come that either played an instrument, danced, sang, did karaoke or was a "jack of all trades" and did a little of everything. If you wanted to see laughter and smiling and singing and clapping of hands and tapping of feet, you should have been there. Patients that you would never have suspected, joined in the fun and had a wonderful time. They may not have talked very well, (some never spoke at all) but somehow or another, words from old songs remembered would be sung with joy. Music does wonders!!!! Feet that could not move well before, all of a sudden had rhythm. It was amazing!!!

PART V

Other Info

CHAPTER 18

THINGS TO PONDER

I have found that when you spend a long period of time with these individuals and repeat, repeat, repeat something… all of a sudden they may totally understand and respond appropriately. It could only last a short time, but it can, and does happen. When you repeat what you said over again slowly, and wait for a response, and repeat it again slowly, and wait for a response and maybe again, a lot of the time you will receive an answer. And if you don't, well….another time will come. Patience is a virtue. The joy you get from their response, because you have waited so long for them to understand you, will be unforgettable. It's like, "gee whiz!!" --he/she finally knows what I was saying. Or, "gee whiz!"-- he/she does know who I am, and…they remembered for that moment.

I have found that when a patient begins to show less interest in eating, if you try to redirect them, or change the subject of eating for just a minute, it may help. For instance, Janice would be escorted to the table for a meal, look at the plate, and say, "I'm not hungry," or "I don't like that, or "I want to go back to my room." If I changed the subject for just a minute, or even turned the plate around so a different view of the food was seen, she would say, "That looks delicious," or "I am really hungry." Of course, there were times that she was escorted back to her room or the family room, but 90% of the time this action was effective. Each individual is different, so you will learn other techniques to encourage them to eat when the time arises.

I have also seen people (not Alzheimer's patients) having a discussion about a particular Alzheimer's patient with "that" patient very close by. To their surprise, the patient understood a good portion of what was being said, and briefly commented on it. This has not only happened once, but several times with different patients. So I implore you, please be very careful what is said in front of them, because they just may be listening and they just may understand exactly what you are saying.

Objects may not be identifiable to them as they are to us. For instance, a cute cuddly teddy bear to us may not be recognized as that by them. A flower that is beautiful may look entirely different to them and not catch their attention. MABEL told me one day when I was showing her a beautiful red rose, "I don't see it as that," and turned around and walked away. I had hoped she would have gotten some kind of enjoyment from it. But that was not the case. I have had others tell me, "That's stupid."

***BERNIE would always sit and look out the window and talk about how beautiful it was out there (looking at the garden of flowers). When I sat with him and talked about the same thing, he was pleased. However, when I mentioned how beautiful the sky was and how clear it was outside, he had no idea what I was talking about. He would say, "Yeah, they are so nice," and point at the garden. When I would try to tell him to look up at the sky, he had no idea what I was talking about. His focus was on something else. So...I made his focus, my focus...and I tried to understand what he was chattering about, from his viewpoint.

They do, however, usually continue to recognize a glass with a drink in it, food on a plate, a cookie or other food if handed to them. However, I have seen some pick up play dough, or a stem from a grape or a tomato, and eat it as if it were delicious. Don't be surprised if when given a book, or a piece of paper with words on it, or even a name badge, they read –out loud-- what they see. I am not sure if they understand what they are reading, but they read the words perfectly.

They are usually attracted to things we would never pay attention to. For instance, a door stopper at a door; a small piece of string hanging from a piece of clothing; a wrinkle in a sheet or blanket; a different color on their blue jeans; a blemish on your face; a button; a dent or scratch on a wall or even an electrical outlet. A beautiful crocheted shawl may catch their attention as something that has "holes all over it".

Be careful with small objects lying around. What is recognizable to us, is not recognizable to them. I have seen patients pick up a tissue and put it in their mouth to eat. They may swallow it, or as some have done, chew on it for a long time until it is rolled up into a saliva saturated ball. As briefly mentioned before, I have also seen them chew a pop top off a metal can, down to a tiny piece of metal the size of a penny. If and when you need to remove an item from their mouth, (even dentures) be careful with your fingers. They have no idea that it will be your finger they are biting down on, and you could lose a finger. Cupping your hand under their mouth and asking them to spit it out has worked multiple times. And again, sometimes it has not.

After a fall, or injury to their head, and/or a trip to the ER, many will remain in bed for 24-48 hours and sleep. Sleep is good for them at this time. The rest and healing process from the injury is vital for their well-being. (Remember, frequent checks are encouraged.) Sometimes, when they finally are able to get up and return to their normal routine, they "seem" to have a clearer mind. By that, I mean they speak sensible words more often, say phrases that make more sense, and seem to follow commands much better. Prior to their injury or fall, they could not. Some even answer a question appropriately. This only lasts for a short time, in some cases, one day, and the patient returns to his pre-fall status. I have no idea why or how this happens, but many of their words, phrases and actions have surprised myself, families and others.

Sundowners---this is a term well known in the medical field. It is usually attributed to a behavior change in a person that will occur late in the afternoon to early evening. That person may become restless, anxious, wander more, or become unsettled in some manner. The behavior he/she exhibits is different from their normal behavior. Providing a calm environment, less noise, re-direction or a one-on-one involvement with that person may help in deterring this change in behavior. This may also be a time to give a medication that helps with calming and relaxation. Your doctor will direct you in this manner.

Medications: Many Alzheimer's patients will have already been placed on some medications by your doctor. The most commonly used medications are used for memory enhancement and to help with clearer thinking. Many patients remain on these medications for several years, and your doctor will advise when they are considered no longer effective. Prior to stopping these, or any other medications, consult your physician. I have seen some medications stopped "early" in the disease process, and a significant, rapid decline was noticed.

There are several medications that are used to help these patients with their behavior, anxiety or sleep. Some patients may do very well with little or no medications. But, there will be those times that something is needed for a certain behavior, whether it be restlessness, a sleep problem, aggressiveness, or depression. I, myself, do not believe in a lot of medications, but I do know that when they are restless, anxious or sad, the feeling they have is very real and uncomfortable to them. If there is something that can be given to them to help ease that feeling, and if used appropriately, I welcome it. If they can't sleep at night, or you can't sleep at night because of their activity, then a mild sleeping pill just might do the trick.

TIP—when using a sleeping pill, please remember that each patient will react differently to medications. There are some patients that are able to walk, but when a problem of sleep occurs and they are placed on a medication, the later effect of the medication can cause them to be unsteady on their feet. If they were to awaken, their potential for falls could be greater. Discuss with your doctor in depth…and always monitor their reaction to any new medications.

We all know that as we age, our muscles and joints become stiffer, and we get those aches and pains that seem to come naturally. If we have a headache, we can go to our cabinet and take an aspirin, or over-the-counter pain aide at our convenience. These people do not have that option. It does not hurt, on occasion, to give them something for minor discomfort. It may relax them and ease their "hurt" when you don't even realize they have a hurt. Talk to your doctor, he is the best one to seek advice from regarding all medications.

TIP: It is amazing how a minor over-the-counter pain relief medication will greatly ease the discomfort, or even anxiety, of one of these lovely people. What does not generally work well with us, offers great and wonderful relief to them.

I, as well as several of my patients' family members, had noticed some interesting behavior and cognitive changes when patients were placed on antibiotics. It does not happen to every patient, and it is not particular to one antibiotic.. but, when some of these patients were on antibiotic therapy, several of them had become more alert, slept less, spoke clearer words and sometimes could almost put words into complete sentences. Prior to the anti-biotic therapy, they could not. This, however, was not long lasting. The patient always reverted back to his/her usual behavior and function. I just thought it was worth mentioning, because this happened many times, and I saw a rebuilding of hope in families, only suddenly to be broken down again. However, looking on a more positive side, those short periods of increased hope also allowed for joy again, even though it was just for a short time. There just might be something to the way certain therapies react to certain patients; and, of course, there may also be a practical explanation to this, but it is not one that I know or understand at this time.

As mentioned before, I have noticed that when one of these patients falls, and has a direct blow to the head, (after returning from the ER) he/she usually recovers after "days" of sleep. There were very few that did not sleep… so it seems that lengthy sleep is a natural need for this trauma. However, when they wake up, they also are more alert and speak clearer than prior to the incident. Again, this does not last for a long time. It may last for only 24-36 hours. I don't know if the sleep has allowed the brain to rest, resulting in clearer speech and thought processes, or if the trauma has done something to the cells in the brain. It's just another perplexing way the body reacts.

CHAPTER 19

UNDERSTANDING THEIR THINKING

***** The following scenarios are actual responses received from patients. Please keep in mind that the "stage" of Alzheimer's affects their response.

***I asked Fred to come sit by me for a while so we could visit. His response was, "I can't sit down. It's not my charge. It's over there." I then led him to a sofa and patted the cushion for him to sit by me. He responded without resistance. When he sat, he said, "This is nice."

***Derrick was restless and walking up and down the halls. This was not his normal behavior. He came up to me as if in terror and said, "Help me find my wife. She left and I am not sure she knows. I tried to tell her, but I have not heard, and I am worried something is wrong." Derrick had not seen his wife for quite a long time. To him, it was like yesterday, and he was becoming very anxious. His feelings were beginning to make his actions escalate. As he was telling me this story, tears were coming down his eyes. I held his hand and asked him to come sit by me. He reluctantly followed, as he kept on saying, "I don't have time. I need her to know now." I told him that I had spoken to her on the phone, and that she knew he would be worried, because he cared so much about her, so she wanted him to know she was ok. I told him that she did not want him to worry, that everything was ok and she would be in touch with him and would explain everything. He accepted this explanation with relief and a huge sigh. His tears stopped and all he could do was hold my hand and tell me over and over again "Thank you, Thank you", and "Yes, she knows I worry," and, "I am glad she called. She doesn't want me with worry. My wife is wonderful". Derrick was totally relieved of his anxiety and distress. I walked him to an area where activity was going on, and he calmly and peacefully joined in.

I saw him the next day and all was forgotten and never mentioned again. I am not one who enjoys telling "stories" to these sweet people, but at the time, I try everything I can to help relieve their distress and bring them to a place of peace. I will do everything I can to help that situation. By focusing on the good things about his wife and her concern for him, his stress was relieved and he became relaxed.

***Josh's eye glasses had been missing for several weeks. When they were finally found in someone else's drawer, they were placed on his face. He did not try to remove them, but when he was asked if they helped him to see better, he replied, "No." I then asked, "Do you see just a little bit better?" He replied, "Not really." I left the glasses on, and after about five minutes had passed, Josh said, "I'm looking for far away that's better." I took this as the glasses had made a difference in his vision. He now wears his glasses every day.

***While Sally was blowing her nose, she was not really sure on how to use the tissue, but finally remembered. After blowing her nose and handing me the tissue, she said, "I need another one, I just blew this one up." She still had some more blowing of her nose that needed to be done.

***Stephanie came up to me one day, very upset and practically crying. She said, "the plesna, is the plesna, and I have to pay for the plesna, even if it had a plesna." She was very anxious and almost frantic. I could not understand what she was trying to tell me, but I knew it was distressing to her. So, I said, "I took care of the plesna and you need not worry anymore." When she looked at me and said, "Are you sure?" I knew I was somewhat on the right track. So I said, "Yes, I am sure." She then grabbed my hand and said, "Thank you, God Bless you," and walked away relieved.

***Tim would stare all day long and just watch others. He would nod on and off to sleep. He never said a word, and usually did not follow any simple instruction. One day while he was sitting and watching others, I noticed his eyes drift towards watching me. I would, at different intervals, go over to him and make small talk, but also say, "I know you hear me, I just wish you would talk to me sometimes." All of a sudden, he said, "I hear you." He smiled peacefully and turned away.

***Jim was an educator in his past. He loved to sit in a recliner and look out the window. There was a remote that controlled the recliner to go up and down next to his chair. One day he started holding the controller up to his mouth, and began mumbling into it. He continued mumbling, with some noticeable words here and there, for about 10 minutes. I can only imagine that he thought it was a microphone and he was giving a presentation. He appeared very content and was confident about what he was saying.

***There were several occasions that some patients would have an episode of anxiety or restlessness, and you could tell something was bothering him/her. However, if at that particular time, a family member arrived, you could see their restlessness change to calmness. The patient did not actually acknowledge or recognize their loved one, but the family's presence made a difference. The patient would sit by the family member, quietly, calm and relaxed, even though very few words were exchanged.

***Patients would be given a snack during mid-day. On this particular day, they were given grapes. I sat down by some of them to do paper work while they ate their snack. Without saying a word, one patient pulled a couple of grapes off the vine, handed me one, as if sharing, and continued eating his grapes. He never looked at me. Likewise, another saw this, then pulled his grapes off and gave me two. How nice. How thoughtful.

***Everyone would sit at a long table to eat lunch. Some were wheeled there in their wheelchairs, others came and sat down after being directed by their caregivers. One day, I said, "Would anyone like to say grace?" Michael folded his hands and bowed his head. I waited for him to say the grace, but he did not. I said the grace and when I opened my eyes, I noticed that several had bowed their heads and folded their hands. He said, "Amen."

***James was sitting in the living room area, looking at a book. I am not sure if he was reading, but he was very engulfed in it. An aide had tried to encourage him to get a shower and a shave, but he was refusing. She came to me and told me he was very confused this morning and was not going to have his A.M. care done. I went over to James and asked him how he was doing. He told me he was fine. I said, "It looks like you are really interested in that book." He told me yes he was. I asked him if it would be all right to set the book aside for a while and get a shower and a nice shave. He told me, "Oh, no. I can't! I have been called for a mission." I asked him, "What kind of a mission?" He stated, "A hostage situation. I can't get a shower and shave because if I were called, I need to leave immediately. That is my duty." I told him I totally understood. I then suggested, "Suppose we skip the shower today, but get a shave. If you are in the shower, there will be no way to get you out of here quickly if you are called, but if we got a shave, we could stop that right away, and you could be on your way." He replied, "Yeah, I can do that. Thanks for understanding." James got his shave. He did not have to respond to his call of duty and the next day he remembered nothing about the hostage situation.

***Jasmine is a lovely little lady that never bothers anyone. She walks and walks most of the day. She speaks very little, but when she sees you she reaches out her hands to you and smiles, then continues on her way. She loves to go into all the rooms and just look around. She has one small habit of picking up things that interest her. One of those things are my papers and notes. There is something about these items that intrigues her. Perhaps papers and notes correlate with her past employment??? Anyway, she had taken my notes and had placed them somewhere. Trying to find out where---was another process. When I was finally "led" to my papers, I hugged Jasmine and laughed with her about our little excursion. Melody, on the other hand was sitting nearby, and whether or not she understood what was going on or not, replied – with bouts of laughter – "I just don't know about you kids!!!"

***Althea was at a stage that all her meals needed to be fed to her. Because she had problems with swallowing, she was now on a pureed diet. She was fed by a teaspoon slowly and carefully. It was noticed that she was beginning to have a problem drinking her regular liquids- ice tea, lemonade, water, etc. For the last few days she was holding the drink in her mouth and not swallowing it for a long time. This day, when she did swallow it, she began to choke. Watching her behavior and actions during meals was very important for her safety. Thickener was added to her drink. Thickener can be purchased at most local pharmacies. It is a substance that gets added to drinks that thickens the drink to a consistency similar to nectar or honey. This added precaution can prevent choking, as well as aspiration. Even though Althea normally did not speak, except for occasional chattering, this day was different. After thickening her drink, and giving her a couple of sips, I said to her, "Isn't that better?" She clearly responded, "Yeah." She continued on thickened liquids.

CHAPTER 20

WHY?

We all question, "Why this disease?" We could also ask, "Why any disease?" There are some things for which we have no answer, and some things we just cannot change....at least for now.

One thing we CAN do is try to deal with it the way it is.......learn to accept it and ....hope for the future. This may seem a little blunt, but if we cannot deal with it, or at least increase our coping abilities and knowledge of the disease, it is going to bring us down. Yes, it is a devastating disease, and yes, our loved one is not how we remember them. The fact remains...this illness is not going to go away-- today. We have to try as hard as we can to learn how to deal with this changed person as best as we can—today. We can either let this disease make our lives miserable, or we can adjust our lives, thoughts, and actions to accept their life as it is now and try to make it better for both. Your loved one will go on...existing in his/her own "little world". They will have good days and bad days and family members will be affected by each. I encourage family members to support each other. If that is not possible, seek support from another place, as it may be too difficult to do on your own. With knowledge and preparation about the signs and symptoms of this disease, you may be able to handle those bad days a little easier.

Remember…your health is at stake, as well. If you can, look for fun times, or good times with your loved one. Reflect on good memories and try to make more good memories from the way they are now. They are still alive…and they still feel. Love them and laugh with them if you can. If they are not smiling, you keep on smiling for them. One day they just may smile or laugh with you. Sometimes they will be fun to watch, and they will do funny things. Remember when your child did something funny or silly, only because of their innocence? You didn't laugh at them to make fun of them. You laughed out of enjoyment. Well, Alzheimer's patients are similar…so go ahead and laugh. Walk with them, talk with them, or just sit by them. Try to get to know them as they are now. I know for a fact that enjoyment can be found. I had it almost every day. But, it is what you make it. Maybe you will be with them at a time when they have that "rainbow moment" (as someone once told me), a time when they remember something from the past and it is verbally shared with you. It will give you more joy than you can possibly imagine. I have seen it happen many times. So, please, as difficult as it may be, try to make the best of it while you can. There are so many bad "things" because of this disease, so try, if you can, to look for the good "things."

EPILOGUE

I have heard it said that Alzheimer's/Dementia affects more than 5 million people in the United States alone, and that this number may more than double by the year 2030 in people over age 65, and many at an earlier age. The risk of developing Alzheimer's increases with age, and they say that one in ten people will develop this disease. New theories now say that some expect one in five (or even more) will be diagnosed with Alzheimer's, even sooner than 2030. With organizations working towards a cure, I can only hope, as many of us do, that someone will find the reason for this debilitating disease, and then find the cure.

I highly recommend that we, those not yet diagnosed with Alzheimer's, keep our bodies in the best condition that we possibly can. If we are going to be that susceptible to this illness, then we should do everything we can, nutritionally, to help our immune system. This may not be the entire answer, but good, pure nutrition can only be of benefit to us in fighting any illness.

Right now, you cannot change the course of the disease, even though there may be new medications that can delay certain stages. But, you CAN change how you look at someone with Alzheimer's. With increased knowledge, you will find certain inner strengths you never realized you had, and it will make it better and easier for them…as well as for yourself. After all, it is not only their care you should be concerned with, but yours, also.

"I know what it is to be in need, and I know what it is to have plenty. I have learned the secret of being content in any and every situation, whether well fed or hungry, whether living in plenty or in want. I can do everything through Him who gives me strength." Philip. 4:12-13 NIV

RESOURCES

National Association of Alzheimer's
1-800-272-3900

Alzheimer's Association
Southeast Florida Chapter
P.O. Box 96011
Washington, DC 20090-6011

INTERNET:
www.alz.org
www.alzfdn.org
www.ahaf.org
www.caregiver.org

National Institute of Mental Health
6001 Executive Boulevard
Room 8184, MSC 9663
Bethesda, MD 20892
301-443-8431
866-615-6464

Alzheimer's Foundation of America
322 Eighth Avenue, 6th Floor
New York, NY 10001
866-232-8484